Just Don't Do It

1,665 Things You Should Never Do

Just Don't Do It

1,665 Things You Should Never Do

By The Lynchsters
with Brendan D. Lynch

1776 Press

Printed in the United States of America. For information, email authorlynch@gmail.com, editor@1776press.com, or contact Bacon Man. Yes, he exists in our minds.

Just Don't Do It: 1,665 Things You Should Never Do
Copyright © 2016
by The Lynchsters with Brendan D. Lynch
ISBN 978-0-9825243-3-6

This is a work of nonfiction (and a little bit of fiction) from the minds of fifth grade students in Mr.Lynch's class. Incidents and places in our book are all ideas from the minds of students. This book will be funny, duh, but in some points we would suggest you don't do any of this because it might not end well. You know, you might end up arrested or something. This book is mostly nonfiction, but some parts are fiction and probably can't actually happen in the real world. Well, maybe they can, but it would be super weird. So don't take most of this book seriously. We have a wide variety of topics from things you shouldn't do at a basketball game to things you shouldn't do in front of your teacher. Our book of *Just Don't Do It: 1,665 Things You Should Never Do* was created and written from the imaginations of 23 fifth grade students. 23 students that are awesome, of course. Have a bacon-filled, scrumptious day!

Printed in the United States of America
1776 Press - Wethersfield, CT

We would like to dedicate this book to the Avon Education Foundation (AEF). Without your grant we would not be published authors. Thank you for funding our book project.

We would also like to dedicate this to Mr. Lynch's future fifth grade classes at Thompson Brook School in Avon, Connecticut. Thank you Mr. Lynch for all of your support and brightening our minds. We will miss you, and you have made an impact on us that we will never forget.

The Lynchsters

Contributing Authors

Mackayla Baxter
Toby Beaudin
Michael Chaho
Danielle Chung
Katelyn Cifaldi
Ravi Corrie
Jae Dolan
Mackenzie Dunn
Christopher Flickinger
Colby Howe
Jack Janes
Cody Lee
Grace Lisle
Jack Marinan
Aidan Namkoong
Emily Nicholas
Charlotte Parry
Benjamin Priest
Ariella Reynolds
Julia Rose
Angelina Schuchardt
Carly Smithberger
Katelyn Wankier

Introduction
By The Lynchsters

Hello and welcome to our super-crazy book! This book started with our amazing teacher, Mr. Lynch, aka Brendan Lynch. We are a bunch of fifth grade students who decided to write a book, and we were able to publish it thanks to Mr. Lynch receiving a grant for almost $1,000 from the Avon Education Foundation. This is an introduction to the book (obviously). We're going to tell you a little about how this all went down. If you ever wished that someone would tell you about a place and what NOT to do when you get there, then you picked up the right book. This book will be funny, and super awesome. (We're not biased. Well, not that much, anyway.) We will talk about summer camps. We will talk about food. We will talk about Mars. And much more! As you can see, these topics are pretty unusual. You will probably like this book. But no promises. Hence the probably. Here's how we wrote this book:

- We spent weeks deciding what to actually write about
- We organized our writing on Google Docs so everyone had access
- We decided to break the book into categories
- We all contributed to the book using Chromebooks in class
- We worked in small teams to handle different parts of the writing
- We worked almost every day (formatting, revising, and editing included)
- We divided up who would write different sections, like this introduction
- We ran an international design contest for the cover
- We voted and gave feedback to the cover designers every day for a week
- We selected a winning cover out of 153 designs
- After many months, we finished on the second to last day of school!

We worked hard on this. We worked at school. We worked at home. It was a lot of work, but it was worth it. We really enjoyed writing everything for you. We hope you love our book and have fun reading it.

A Few Final Thoughts...
By Brendan D. Lynch

First and foremost, I did not write this book - my students did. Consider me their coach. Or overlord. Yes, overlord. That makes me sound powerful, like I live in a castle and eat dinner wearing my velvet robe. Anyway, students were the decision makers in every single aspect of the process, from deciding what to write to exactly how the cover looked. By the way, fifth graders are some serious graphic design critics. If they didn't like how a font was angled they made it sound like the designer should be immediately sent to a prison work camp. As their overlord, my job was to keep the task realistic. To veer them away from ideas that might be cool, but also problematic. You know, like adding a feature that shocks the readers with electricity on page 19.

For most authors, the hardest part of writing a book is actually writing the book. I always tell my students that everyone has a bestselling book idea in their heads, but few act on that and take the time to write. However, this project had a huge advantage - 23 authors. The challenge was coming up with a project that 23 authors could work on at the same time, without compromising consistency. It took over a week of discussion and voting to narrow it down to a theme/topic that everyone would enjoy, but would also be manageable.

Even with so many authors, the process was extremely time consuming and took several months. Teams were put together to check, recheck, and check again all the entries that other teams worked on. Revise, revise, revise. They wrote the introduction, the author page, the dedication page, and even the copyright page. The title, font choices, and even the actual color of the pages (creme vs. white) were all decisions they had to debate and vote on. The only page I wrote is the one you are reading right now. Using grant money, we ran a design contest with a $500 prize that brought in designers from all over the world. Each day for a week, students took out their Chromebooks, analyzed the designs as they rolled in, and gave feedback. The designers took this feedback, made changes, and at the end of the week the students voted on the final design.

We finished everything with about 24 hours to go before their summer vacation began. The end result of their hard work is the book you are now holding in your hands. This would not have been possible without the dedication and perseverance of 23 awesome kids. Enjoy.

While Introducing Yourself

Sneeze and then shake the person's hand

Speak in a fake British accent

Say that the person's face looks weird

Lick your hand and then shake someone else's

Speak in a fake language

Start vigorously picking your nose

Only whisper or yell

Sweat a lot

Give the person a pat on the head

Throw up on the person's feet

Speak only with made-up hand signals

Pretend your name is Captain Bakamatador

Kiss the person on the forehead

Say "sup" and slap the person on the back

Pretend you are allergic to the person

At a Private Beach

Dig gigantic holes and cover them with towels

Leave without all of your things

Drink ocean water

Invite people to a party on someone else's beach

Eat seafood that is still moving

Kick sand at other people

Bring annoying kids

Leave garbage on the beach

Bring pets off leash

Go swimming during a shark feeding frenzy

Throw a beach ball into a little kid's face

Pull out someone's umbrella

Play loud music that no one likes

Tell the beach's owner that the sand is dirty

Steal people's picnic lunches

On Vacation

Yell at the lifeguards

Get kicked out of a resort

Ride your bike in the hallways of a hotel

Ask the front desk employee annoying questions

Jump in the elevator

Get in a fight with the maid

Bump into a person that you don't know

Do Zumba in the hotel lobby

Jump in the pool from the roof

Say "Hi mom" to someone who is not your mom

Hold up a metal pole when there's lightning

Take the clean towels and throw them in the pool

Step on a pufferfish

Ask strangers for directions to the torture chamber

Poke sharks in the nose

In the Library

Throw food

Start a book fight

Yell

Eat food while reading

Run around

Talk back to the librarian

Put a book down on its spine

Laugh very obnoxiously from a book

Bring a kid into adult section

Read on your phone

Destroy the computers

Complain because you cannot find a book

Say you don't want to be here to librarian

Lose your book and don't pay overdue fine

Take out all copies of the same book

In the Woods

Poke a bear

Eat weird mushrooms you find on the ground

Eat random plants

Attack a tree

Eat sketchy berries

Try to touch a fluffy raccoon

Touch random plants

Hug poison ivy

Dress up like a deer during hunting season

Touch an animal foaming at the mouth

Climb up the tallest tree and jump

Eat glowing blueberries

Rub yourself with bark

Use soap as shampoo

Lay in a log that's next to a cliff

At Home

Put a pile of metal forks in the microwave

Invite the entire school over for a party

Eat expired food

Play with fire

Put your siblings' electronics in the shower

Talk back to your parents

Let skunks inside

Leave food in your parents' bed

Turn on the blender when the cap isn't on

Crawl in the chimney when the fireplace is on

Let in a scary clown

Throw rocks at your window

Try to get out of doing homework

Eat a lot of cookies

Leave the shower on all day

At a Baseball Game

Throw food at the players

Drink five bottles of soda

Swallow peanut shells

Go on the field while the game is on

Fight to catch the ball

Throw the ball back at the player's back

Annoy the players

Fight with the other team

Be a bad sport

Try to get hit by the ball

Get up in down in the stands

Scream at both teams

Be an obnoxious fan

Be a Yankees and Red Sox fan

Hit the baseball back on the field with a bat

At Sleep Away Camp

Escape on the first night

Spit at people in your cabin

Stay up the entire night

Annoy your counselor

Be mean to your cabin mates

Let bears into your cabin

Forget to shower

Eat other kids' snacks

Prank the counselor

Order anchovy pizza delivery for other cabins

Go to the woods with a friend and leave him there

Pour laundry detergent in the pool

Sleep on the roof of the cabin

Try to sneak in a big screen television

Collect insects and store them in your bed

On the Road

Spill coffee on yourself

Go triple the speed limit

Text while driving

Drive without a seatbelt

Get road rage at police officers

Yell "This guy is kidnapping me" out your window

Stick your head out the window like a dog

Kick the seat in front of you

When someone falls asleep color on them

Run over shopping carts

Drive on sidewalks

Watch a movie in another car while driving

Put chocolate on your seat in the summer

Fall asleep while driving

Drive with door open

While Playing Sports

Forget your equipment on purpose

Cheat on every play

Kick a ball at the coach

Be a sore loser

Not shake hands with other team

Tell your teammates what to do

Brag how amazing you are at everything

Roll in the grass like a dog

Yell at your coach in a made up language

Sing opera in the middle of the game

Wear a scary mask during the game

Mess the field up after it has been cleaned

Eat corn on the cob while playing in the game

Run around the field when a game is going on

Tie all of your teammates' shoes together

When You're Hungry

Eat household plants

Stuff your mouth with your entire plate of food

Keep complaining about how you're hungry

Eat everything in the house

Take bites from everyone else's food

Take food from babies

Eat spoonfuls of sugar

Have a temper tantrum

Eat a snack bigger than your dinner

Dig through the trash can for food

Eat your toys

Say you can't do anything because you're hungry

Call the police

Run into walls

Threaten the refrigerator

On a Military Base

Push the Red Button

Yell at a general

Do the opposite of what you're supposed to do

Blow up the dynamite

Steal a tank

Call an officer "dude"

Have a fist fight with a poster of Uncle Sam

Call your mom because you are scared

Ask for money

Aim at someone

Steal a plane

Sneeze on a general

Yell gibberish at other soldiers

Demand tacos

Jump on a random soldier's back

In a Bank

Ask for $1,000 in pennies

Wear a ski mask

Yell at the security guard

Take a lot of bank candy

Demand money

Wave around a water gun

Use someone else's bank account

Withdraw too much money

Throw your change on the ground

Pinch the security guard's cheeks

Look suspicious

Wander into random offices

Use someone else's password

Trade in a 100 dollar bill for quarters

Throw marbles on the floor

In the Principal's Office

Sing nursery rhymes

Break things on the principal's desk

Jump on the principal's desk

Argue for no reason

Pretend you didn't do anything

Go to sleep on the floor

Be a wise guy

Yell at the principal

Smack your lip loudly

Have a temper tantrum

Throw things at the window

Play video games on your phone

Blame an animal

Roll your eyes

Hop around the office like a kangaroo

At a Ski Resort

Jump off the chair lift

Pretend your ski poles are light sabers

Stand on the chair

Push someone off the chair lift

Yell at toddlers to ski faster

Refuse to show your ski pass

Forget to get off the lift

Throw your skis in the woods

Ski over other people's skis

Eat dirty snow

Wear shorts when it's freezing

Text while skiing

Look down

Refuse to sit with people wearing red coats

Sit on someone's lap on the lift

During Thanksgiving

Eat before dinner starts

Jump in the mashed potatoes

Start a conga line through the kitchen

Refuse to eat anyone's food

Be mean to your family members

Be ungrateful

Double dip everything

Feed the dog your vegetables

Start a food fight with your grandparents

Drink the gravy

Put your fingers in the cranberry sauce

Mix milk and soda together

Break all the plates

Unplug the television during the football game

Take both of the drumsticks

At the Pool

Drink the pool water

Dive in the low end

Dance on diving board

Make the life guard keep rescuing you

Run everywhere

Eat in the pool

Wear your shoes in the pool

Bring a giant duckie float on the waterslide

Wear an electric bathing suit

Do a backflip when you don't know how to

Forget to put on sunscreen

Pretend you're drowning

Throw sand in the pool

Play marco polo by yourself

Put fish in the pool

At a Farm

Feed animals human food

Jump over a fence

Yell at an animal

Chase chickens

Let the animals eat all the food

Scream loudly to startle the animals

Ride a chicken

Eat ham in front of the pigs

Stick your finger in a bunny's mouth

Stand behind a horse

Take selfies with the animals

Ride a horse without a saddle

Let an animal loose

Act like the animals' prey

Make fun of the animals

At the Beach

Throw sand at other people

Go in the water when there is a red flag

Chase after sharks

Stick your hand in a conch shell

Go fishing around other people

Put food on your head for the seagulls

Kick a soccer ball at people

Walk on slippery rock

Touch a jellyfish

Walk across a fishing line

Pick up a dead fish

Throw rocks at the seagulls

Kiss a jellyfish

Swim in a lightning storm

Go on a leaky boat

During a Job Interview

Cough and sneeze all over the interviewer

Say you dislike the job

Say you are slightly evil

Admit you are lazy

Chew a giant wad of gum

Fall asleep

Start playing a video game on your phone

Call your mom

Say you like to steal candy from babies

Start talking about your love life

Stand on the interviewer's desk

Say that your don't have any interest in the job

Pull out a sandwich and start eating it

Have bad breath

Start crying

In Front of Your Crush

Pick your nose

Sneeze on the person

Have seaweed breath

Drool all over yourself

Do something weird in front of their parents

Start crying over a dead mosquito

Roll in mud

Stare at them

Start whispering when they enter the room

Pass gas

Burp

Sing Happy Birthday to yourself

Juggle sushi

Say you have an amazing tricycle

Lie to impress them

In a Bowling Alley

Run down the lane

Text while bowling

Drop the ball on your foot

Slide down the bowling alley

Steal other people's shoes

Bowl in someone else's lane

Throw the bowling ball at somebody

Chuck a bowling ball at the screen/tv

Play catch with the bowling ball

Run laps in the bowling alley

Have different sized shoes on

Throw the bowling ball in the bathroom

Spend all your time at the vending machine

Try to bounce the bowling ball

Throw a shoe at someone

In a Museum

Take a photo when it says no

Touch the artifacts

Pretend you are part of the museum

Run around the museum

Tug on the red rope

Knock things over

Run down the staircases

Ride on the animal statues

Bother the security guards

Set off alarm on purpose

Break ancient artifacts

Take money from the tip jar

Steal from the gift shop

Ignore important signs

Ride down a stair banister

In Front of the President

Tell the president your parents didn't vote

Read the president's notes

Steal the president's favorite pen

Add parts to the president's speech

Spill juice in the Oval Office

Put your feet on the president's desk

Yell at the president

Tell what you don't like about the White House

Steal souvenirs from the Oval Office

Try to sing the president a lullaby

Annoy the Secret Service

Ask a lot of obnoxious questions

Pretend the president's couch is a trampoline

Keep asking where the swimming pool is

Jump on his desk

While Grocery Shopping

Throw food out of the cart

Get in on top of the groceries

Sit in the baby seat

Eat food before paying for it

Pretend the cart is a surfboard

Do parkour in the store aisles

Sing on the intercom

Open the food without buying it

Ask the butcher to cut meat then walk away

Leave your money on the floor

Take food out of other people's cart

Leave without paying

Ride on the shopping cart like a maniac

Sit in the middle of the aisle and play video games

Pour milk on unsuspecting customers

On a Bike Ride

Stand on your bike seat

Ride off the path

Ride into little kids

Zigzag around other riders

Ride in the middle of the road

Curb surf

Stop in the middle of the road to talk to your friend

Pretend your bike is a bumper car

Drive in front of a car

Ring the bell at everyone you pass

Try to eat tacos while riding

Fall off on purpose

Have biker road rage

Do wheelies in traffic

Hijack someone's bike

In Front of Your Teacher

Say bad words

Whine / cry

Chew gum and stick it on the teacher's desk

Pass notes

Eat loudly when they're talking

Sing during a test

Pick your nose

Moan that your hair hurts

Drop food on the floor / carpet

Drool on your desk

Stand on your chair

Play eraser soccer

Stand on your desk and dance

Throw paper airplanes at the wall

Sharpen your pencil once every five minutes

On the Bus

Run up and down the aisle

Jump over the seats

Dance in the aisles

Sing annoying songs

Bang on the windows

Stick your foot out for people to trip

Ask the bus driver odd questions

As the driver for money

Open and close the windows over and over

Leave wrappers on the ground

Wave to every car that passes

Run to the front and change the radio station

Pull the fire alarm for no reason

Open the rear door while moving

Leave garbage on the floor

To Animals

Ride them (unless they're a horse)

Make them eat things they don't want to eat

Paint them pink

Make them wear ugly clothes

Give them a wet willy

Bite them

Go close to their faces

Drop them

Eat them

Name them silly names

Give them too many baths

Put perfume or cologne on them

Make them wear sneakers

Hurt them

Lay on top of them

While At Work

Talk to people when they are on the phone

Spill a drink on the paper you are working on

Eat food over your paper and make crumbs

Be late for work

Run in the office

Do yoga on your desk

Annoy your boss

Try and get fired

Pretend that you have a master's degree in bowling

Talk back to the boss

Bring in your pet rat

Draw bad pictures of your boss

Drink other people's coffee

Answer the phone in a made-up language

Play games on your computer all day

At the Aquarium

Stick your finger in a shark's mouth

Throw candy corn into the tanks

Go swimming with piranhas

Read poetry to dolphins

Get lost in the aquarium

Stick your face in the tank

Pet a jellyfish

Feed an animal that you're not supposed to

Pretend you're a flopping fish

Eat food off the ground

Throw a baseball at the glass

Pour soda in the tank

Ask the tour guide to leave

Dip your toes in a fish tank

Run after a penguin

While Playing Video Games

Throw your remote at the TV

Push the buttons so hard that your finger breaks

Break the buttons before you buy the controller

Skip school to play games

Don't eat or drink because you are so addicted

Play constantly for multiple days

Throw the remote at a window

Yell "Only one more round!" over and over again

Forget to go to school

Get addicted to a game

Rage quit

Draw on the TV

Play a M rated game when you're too young

Ignore the real world

If you lose, break everything

In a Different Country

Start a rebellion

Drive on wrong side of the road

Leave the restaurant without paying

Ask someone for directions

Speak the wrong language

Pay with the wrong country's money

Lose your passport

While trying to speak their language say a bad thing

Eat an insanely hot pepper by accident

Get arrested

Lose your luggage

Insult their culture

Get lost

Lie to the police

Lose your room key

In a Fancy Restaurant

Start a food fight

Wear sweatpants

Go into the kitchen

Yell at the waiter

Start a fire

Put your feet on the table

Give the waiter/waitress no tip

Yell at the other diners

Set off the fire alarm

Pay in pennies

Talk about going to another restaurant

Leave without paying

Color on the table

Eat something that has a hair

Ask for fries

During a Wedding

Dress exactly like the bride

Eat the cake before you're supposed to

Open the gifts if you're not the bride or groom

Run down the aisle

Hit people with the flowers

Lose the ring

Yell "I object to everything" at the ceremony

Trip while walking down the aisle

Drop the rings

Play inappropriate songs while going down the aisle

Sit on the tables

Say you don't like the bride's dress

Yell during the ceremony

Smash the cake

Tell the bride and groom their marriage is doomed

At a Graduation Party

Sneeze on all the food

Lose your diploma

Use your graduation robe as a tissue

Make people smell your shoes

Tell everyone it's your birthday when it's no

Give everyone awkward hugs

Tell everyone you cheated on every test

Pretend to be someone else

Say you fell asleep during a lecture

Hit someone with your hat

Start a soccer game in your house

Try to sneak out the back door

Lie about what degree you received

Skip out on your own party

Use your graduation cap as a plate

In a Barber Shop

Shake your head while the barber is using a razor

Eat the hair on the floor

Try to cut your own hair

Yell at the person that has the razor in there hand

Put every product in your hair

Dance in your seat

Set off the fire detector

Move when the barber has scissors

Get the razor gelled into your hair

Eat the hair products

Cut in front of people

Pick up the hair on the ground and take it home

Take the scissors and cut your own hair

Ask for an uneven cut

Run out without paying

At the Mall

Look sketchy and suspicious

Rearrange furniture in a furniture store

Ride a quad through the mall

Scream and shout at children

Rob a store

Spray water at a security guard

Start a fight in front of strangers

Tell random people you hate their shoes

Annoy store employees

Hit the fire alarm

Start a dance mob

Eat other restaurants' food in other restaurants

Forget to pay

Follow another parent around

Try on all the clothes without buying anything

On a Boat

Jump off a boat when there is jellyfish under you

Push someone off the boat

Let a dolphin get stuck in the fishing net

Try to be bit by a shark

Poke holes in the boat

Jump into the water and bring someone with you

Go over a rock pile

Take control of the boat when no one knows

Let go of your hat

Bump into the dock

Run out of gas

Drive the boat into a sand bar

Let a king salmon pull you in the water

Throw trash overboard

Pour water in the boat until it sinks

On a Plane

Not put your seatbelt on

Go in the aisle when the seatbelt sign is on

Do jumping jacks

Snore loudly

Lie on the person's shoulder that is next to you

Laugh really loud over and over

Have the tray down when the plane is taking off

Get in a karate fight with another passenger

Kick the seat in front of you

Go in the aisle when they are handing out snacks

Use the word "bomb" in a sentence

Run sprints down the aisle

Poke the person next to you

Keep knocking on the pilot's door

Climb on the plane's wing

At a Carnival

Step in animal droppings

Steal prizes

Spend all your money in the first five minutes

Get mad at rides

Pop little kids' balloons

Cheat at games

Jump off the ferris wheel

Throw a baseball at a vendor

Yell gibberish at random people

Eat too much cotton candy

Fall asleep on a ride

Lay on the tracks of a roller coaster

Jump into the ring

Get mad because you didn't get a pink unicorn

Try to become part of a carnival game

At a Tennis Tournament

Tell your team that they are not very good

Scream if you don't get the trophy

Say that something was out if it wasn't

Try to use your hand as a racket

Be a sore loser

Jump over the net

Throw your racket at the other team

Help the other team by giving them advice

Cry if you miss a ball

Text while playing a set

Sing loudly during the match

Slice every shot

Call your team "pink fluffy unicorn"

Brag if you win

Air slap at the other team if you lose

During a Meditation Session

Talk loudly

Play on your phone

Play football

Ask why people are doing this

Hum loudly

Say that "finding chi" is dumb

Scream at your imaginary friends

Say that meditation is boring

Do jumping jacks

Annoy the other meditators

Do pushups

Snore

Dress up like Darth Vader

Fall asleep and start snoring

Bring a messy snack and chew it loudly

At a Spelling or Geography Bee

Say you hate spelling

Ask how to spell a word

Spell in a different language

Faint

Sing the words

Say the opposite of what you were going to say

Cry if you miss a letter

Throw a temper tantrum if you lose

Pull a map out of your pocket at geography bee

Refuse to speak

Annoy the judges

Yell at the judge because you got something wrong

Act like the smartest person ever to live

Mess up, and then run off the stage

Bring a dictionary

On Top Of a Tree

Break the branch that you're sitting on

Cover yourself in sap

Drop something heavy on the person beneath you

Hang upside down and fall down

Get stuck up in the tree and need to be rescued

Get your pet stuck up in the tree

Hang upside down and get stuck

Pull off the leaves and branches

Push the person that you're sitting with off the tree

Drill a giant hole in the tree

Jump into a hole

Jump on the branches

Pick all the apples and throw them at people

Play with the squirrels

Pick off all the bark

At a Party

Break the first thing you see

Stay up all night on a school night

Drink the pool water

Attract the police with your noise

Party when the hosts' parents aren't home

Fall asleep in a bed that is not yours

Go wild

Eat other people's food

Prank call the police

Party during the school day

Ruin the party

Text on other peoples' phones

Eat random foods you find in the cabinet

Steal their shampoo

Invite a bad band

When Someone Else Is Reading

Ask unnecessary questions

Spoil the ending of the book

Offer them food

Make them read the book aloud

Yell in their ear

Tie their shoes together

Spill water on their book

Ask them if you can read the book right now

Spoil the plot of the book

Start playing with their hair

Read the same book aloud

Rip the book out of their hands

Sit uncomfortably close to them

Tell them the latest celebrity drama

Laugh at them

At a Waterpark

Wear a tuxedo

Go down a slide the wrong way

Jump off a ride while it's moving

Try to knock someone else off the ride

Be rude to the people working there

Pop someone else's raft

Be mean to your friend in front of your parents

Clog water pipes with used gum

Turn off the water switch

Cut people in line

Bring sharp items on rides with rafts

Eat food in the water

Throw trash/litter in the water

Pour soda down a waterslide

Push people out of the way

During Winter

Jump in the snow with your bathing suit on

Throw a snowball at a cop

Eat yellow snow

Skate on thin ice

Throw an ice ball near a car window

Walk on a pond filled with slush

Stick your tongue to a frozen pole

Bury someone in the snow, and leave them

Sled near a rock wall

Lick the salt on the roads

Stand in front of a snow plow

Swim outside

Build an igloo with no exit

Eat sand on the road

Put pepper on driveway instead of salt

At Grandma's House

Wear her jewelry

Eat all of her cookies

Jump on her bed

Try to get a piggy back ride

Unplug her TV

Use her toothbrush

Tell her you did not like the dinner she made

Ask to go shopping and buy everything

Tell her that her apple pie is terrible

Put your smelly feet on her couch

Ask her a lot of questions about pudding

Play football in her living room

Eat all of her butterscotch

Walk in the house with muddy shoes

Color on her countertops

In an Airport

Drink a lot of water before you get on the plane

Go on the wrong plane

Stand in the runway

Pick up the wrong luggage

Follow the wrong person

Call a police officer by their first name

Keep using the word "bomb" in conversation

Follow a different family

Annoy the security guards

Get on the luggage conveyor belt

Bring a gallon of water in your carry-on luggage

Wear a lot of metal to mess with the metal detector

Run a 5k race in the hallways

Keep ice cream in your suitcase

Try to stuff yourself in a suitcase

In the Bathroom

Leave the toilet unflushed

Leave toilet paper all over the ground

Flood the toilet and not tell anyone

Leave the sink on

Put tons of soap in the sink so that it can't wash out

Use all the toilet paper

Spray so much air freshener that you can't breath

Leave the hair dryer on full blast

Leave the shower on with the drain closed

Leave the bath running

Turn on the shower too hot

Use the hand dryer to dry your hair

Clog the toilet and don't unclog it

Pour bubble bath in the sink

Pull the assistance rope when you don't need it

At Laser Tag

Don't wear the proper gear

Wear no vest

Forget what team you are on

Start shooting non-stop

Forget how to shoot the laser

Throw your laser gun at people

Slither on the ground like a snake

Run into a wall while running

Shoot your own teammates

Spin in circles and get dizzy

Pull other kids' hair

Stop and eat a bowl of cereal while playing

Shoot someone in the eye

Bring a bowling bowl into the laser tag room

Wear clothes that glow

In New York

Talk to every stranger you see

Eat gum from the sidewalk

Get lost

Take money from street collection jars

Follow the wrong person

Hug a stranger

Get on the wrong bus

Walk into the wrong apartment

Get on the wrong train/subway

Throw pennies off of tall buildings

Climb the Statue of Liberty

Go into dark and scary alleys

Run away from your parents

Lose your friends in the subway

Eat all the free samples

In the Kitchen

Rub germs on the silverware

Spit in all the food

Eat food until you throw up

Let your pet eat people food

Bang all the pots and pans together

Play with all the knives

Put all the refrigerated food in the cabinets

Play tackle football with a loaf of bread

Lick all the food

Make a castle out of sugar and flour

Leave the refrigerator door open

Spray ketchup on the windows

Forget to put the lid on the blender

Boil soda on the stove

Eat dessert before dinner

During a Holiday

Attack people with light sabers

Pick pocket your guests

Start a food fight

Go into rage mode

Tell them you hate their gift to you

Eat the turkey before it's cooked

Scream because you have to stay and talk at dinner

Tell your relatives they smell

Set the house on fire

Spit when you talk

Sample the food before it's ready

Put ants in people's purses

Try to scare small children

Ignore everyone

Stuff your face with food

On a Date

Pretend you forgot to bring money

Stare at your date, not saying anything

Go use the bathroom every two minutes

Pick your nose

Fake laugh at everything

Say something rude about them

Lie about your job

Spill sauce on their clothes

Sneeze on them

Make awkward noises

Lie about everything

Talk with your mouth full

Have bad manners

Eat super smelly food

Stuff your mouth with food

In Prison

Fight the big people

Escape through a lit chimney

Climb the wall to get out

Spit at your cellmate

Make the guards mad at you

Wear a suit to every meal

Tell the other inmates they smell

Try to dig a tunnel with a plastic spoon

Steal people's shoes

Upset the strong prisoners

Visit a criminal that you don't know

Step inside a cell without a guard

Tell the cooks their food is nasty

Wake up all the other inmates with opera

Threaten your cellmate with a water gun

At The Dinner Table

Say that you don't like the food

Kick your siblings under the table

Bring electronics to the table

Invite friends to dinner without asking your parents

Eat dessert before dinner

Chew with your mouth open

Spit out food onto the table if you don't like it

Complain that you didn't get enough dessert

Kick the table

Sneak food to your pets

Throw away your vegetables

Yell at your family

Breathe on people's faces after eating garlic

Interrupt family members when they're talking

Leave before dinner is done

In The Classroom

Make a bad first impression with everyone

Start to fight with your friend in front of the class

Call your teacher "mommy" or "daddy"

Cry because you broke a pencil

Look at another student's test

Throw pencils

Fall asleep during a lesson

Drop food on the carpet

Bring in glitter if your teacher hates glitter

Start your own class

Leave a mess at the end of the day

Steal pencils

Throw up in your desk

Break something important

Ask the teacher inappropriate questions

In The Cafeteria

Start a food fight

Use all your lunch money on the first day

Leave a mess

Not eat your food

Throw all your food away

Insult the cafeteria workers about their food

Take the last bag of chips

Don't recycle

Exclude people from your table

Shoot straw wrappers out of your straw

Eat peanuts in front of someone allergic to them

Spray juice at everyone

Insult people's food choices

Throw away your tray

Don't pay the right amount

While Watching TV

Press random buttons on remote

Pour water on the TV

Use the screen as a target

Stare at the TV when it's not on

Leave the TV on over night

Get mad and throw something at the screen

Leave it on a channel that doesn't work

Hog the remote

Fire a water gun at the TV

Watch a channel that you shouldn't watch

Put a foot through the screen

Complain that you don't get to watch enough TV

Invite friends over to watch TV then ignore them

Scratch the screen

Stand in front of the screen doing jumping jacks

At a Supermarket

Climb on the shelves

Open a box of cereal and pour it on the floor

Run around and get lost

Lock yourself in a freezer

Fill a bunch of carts with food and leave them full

Get cupcakes and throw them on the wall

Make the checkout person pay for your food

Shake all the soda bottles

Eat all the candy in the checkout area

Open something and leave it on ground

Ride on the shopping cart

Ask the cashier to give you a piggyback ride

Shoplift

Give the cashier a penny and ask for change

Sample from the salad bar

During Recess

Run into a pole

Refuse to line up

Set the field on fire

Run into the woods

Be a bully

Eat grass

Sneak inside the school

Jump off the swing into a pole

Eat the red berries

Exclude people

Eat dirt

Play with bugs

Sit in the corner and cry

Be a poor sport

Tell on someone for nothing

In Front of a Young Child

Stick your finger in an electrical outlet

Yell at your phone

Eat toys

Let them eat napkins

Teach them how to play with fire

Make them do your homework

Let them explore a deep lake on their own

Let them set off fireworks

Fight with strangers

Tell them to go play in the road

Tell them there is a monster under their bed

Teach little kids things that they don't need to learn

Throw your popcorn in a movie theater

Be inappropriate

Run around a pool

On Public Property

Throw eggs at buildings

Paint graffiti on everything

Rip up the grass with shovels

Litter

Build your house on land that is already taken

Toilet paper the trees

Break the security cameras

Make something dirty and not clean up

Cut down a tree

Dig a hole for someone to fall in

Pick all of the petals off of a flower

Eat the flowers

Make a tree fort

Paint everything pink

Dig a gigantic hole and fill it with water

In the Wild

Eat weird looking berries

Harm a skunk

Bring a boat with no water to put it in

Bring a fake knife

Sleep without a shelter

When it's cold forget to tend to the fire

Light the woods on fire

Pet a porcupine

Leave your marshmallows on over night

Tie meat to you and run around

Forget to close the door to your tent/shelter

Kill animals for no reason

Sleep in a bed of poison ivy

Hug a skunk

Step on a poisonous frog

At a Train Station

Cross the yellow line

Go to the bathroom when your train is coming

Run on the train tracks

Stand on top of a train

Get stuck in between the doors

Go to the conductor's room and pull the horn

Miss the step

Stand on the side of the train

Backflip off the top of the train

Hijack the train

Miss your train

Start a riot while waiting for your train to arrive

Spill coffee on people

Tell everyone that trains are unsafe

Take pictures of strangers without their permission

While Sledding

Go sledding in the road

Push the person that is sledding off the sled

Go sledding in the dark

Crash into houses

Sled backwards

Go off of a jump with a broken sled

Jump off the sled while it's in the air

Leave the sledding hill without your sled

Grease the bottom of your sled with olive oil

Sled in the summer

Text while sledding

Put too many people on a sled

Sled into a thorn bush

Stand on your sled while it's moving

Eat tacos

At a Concert

Throw your instrument

Play the wrong notes

Drop your instrument

Talk loudly to everyone

Interrupt the entire show

Put food in other people's instruments

Kick all the props

Get out of your seat and attack the conductor

Yell in the microphone

Run around on stage

Wave to everyone you know

Throw things at the audience

Crawl on stage

Start to laugh hysterically

Text while playing

At a Parade

Jump on a parade float

Boo all of the dancers

Try to sneak into the parade

Do cartwheels in front of performers

Take off performers' masks

Yell at people for candy

Make a float shaped like a piranha

Start a riot

Pop a parade float

Run circles around a group of dancers

Walk across the road

Drive through when the parade is going on

Play loud music from your car nearby

Play football in the middle of the parade

Try to block the parade with orange cones

At a Play

Talk on your phone

Run up on the stage and hug an actor

Lay down on the stage in the middle of the play

Throw food on the stage

Take pictures with a flash

Text while watching the play

Kick the seat in front of you

Run up and down the aisles

Fall asleep and snore loudly

Use the bathroom every five minutes

Yawn during a sad scene

Spill water on the ground

Boo the actors

Chew something really loudly

Clap when you're not supposed to

At a Store

Eat all the free samples

Speak on the loudspeaker

Keep ringing the bell for service

Turn on all the electronics

Don't pay for anything

Climb the shelves

Put on all the makeup in the beauty aisle

Throw flour on other customers

Crack all of the eggs

Run in the aisles

Take money from charity jars

Think everything is free

Lock yourself in the freezer

Put pudding on yourself and run through the store

Play inappropriate music on the loudspeaker

At the Drive-thru

Go through the drive-thru multiple times

Say how much you dislike the restaurant

Ask for 17 packets of ketchup

Try to crawl through the window

Tell a long story

Try to pay with Monopoly money

Throw darts at the window

Pull up to wrong area

Order things they don't have

Say that working at a drive-thru is a bad job

Talk about personal things

Ask if you can have their phone number

Sing to the drive-thru person

Whistle your order

Play your radio really loud while you order

At School

Hide in the woods at recess

Cut the lunch line

Talk when you are supposed to be reading

Walk the mile

Not follow the dress code

Eat snack right when you get to school

Make enemies

Swear

Start a fight

Spill your water bottle on a test

Hide in a locker

Pretend you're sick

Do parkour on the lockers

Ride a skateboard down the hall

Call your teachers by their first name

Mars

Eat the red rocks

Take off your helmet

Forget to wear a spacesuit

Let yourself float away

Throw rocks at the spaceship

Poke a hole in your spacesuit

Accidentally hit the "self destruct" button

Annoy the aliens

Go in a UFO without knowing where it's going

Leave a man behind on Mars when you leave

Get stuck on Mars

Set the inside of your spaceship on fire

Go outside in a meteor shower

Lose your connection to Earth

Go into space in a tarp

At a Petting Zoo

Place your hand in the alligator exhibit

Try to steal the ponies

Yell at the animals

Place your hand in a dark hole

Eat food without washing your hands

Climb in the tiger cage

Feed the animals too much food

Sit on a porcupine

Feed the animals fast food

Steal a poisonous snake

Jump in the piranha tank

Lick your fingers after petting the animals

Feed the animals lollipops

Drop a tarantula on the ground

Taunt the animals

During Hide And Seek

Look when you count

Never come out

Go inside a building

Quit in the middle of the game

Stomp your feet so that people know where you are

Sing nursery rhymes while you're hiding

Count too quickly

Go inside and eat dinner

Climb up a 100-foot tree

Go on vacation

Get caught and hide again

Tell someone where the other person hid

Start fights

Take a nap

Stay in your hiding spot overnight

During a Contest

Make a big deal about losing

Pretend you are the winner

Be a sore loser

Scream that the contest rules were unfair

Get carried out by security

Brag and yell in someone's face when you win

Cheat

Switch your bronze medal for someone's gold

Have a meltdown

Steal the trophy or medal from the winner

Use your phone to find the answers

Gloat if you win

Brag about your trophy

Tell everyone that you are better than them

Say that the judges were unfair

During a Natural Disaster

Go outside

Forget your kids if you are a parent

Loot stores

Run into a tornado

Play football in a hurricane

Throw your sibling into a tornado

Walk on the beach as a tsunami is coming

Sit at the edge of an active volcano

Stand in the way of an avalanche

Sell people fake disaster relief kits

Scream "Sacrifices must be made!"

Don't share food

Panic

Peacefully gaze at the sky when a tornado is coming

Run slowly because you are eating food

On a Snowy Mountain

Cause an avalanche

Fall off the mountain

Drop your phone off of a cliff

Eat strangely colored snow

Sled down the iciest part

Try to melt the snow with your breath

Hold up the line to take pictures

Fall into an endless crevice

Chew on frozen tree branches

Ski on someone's feet

Try to do a jump and fail

Wear no jacket

Slide down the mountain

Push someone over the edge

Take off your gloves on a cold day

During a Surfing Lesson

Start surfing in really shallow water

Fail a surfing test

Jump off every time

Surf into a shark

Get a cut and attract "big fish"

Surf in deep water when you can't swim or surf

Use an inflatable surfboard

Try to surf in a calm pond

Wrap your legs around the surfboard

Forget how to swim

Surf/Swim with chum (shark bait)

Drink the salt water

Yell at your instructor

Try to do tricks on your board for the first time

Swim away from the group

At a Lake

Pretend you're a shark

Splash people reading on the beach

Run laps around the perimeter

Hit your head on the dock while jumping in

Fake a heart attack

Jump in the deep end if you can't swim

Swim between people's legs

Pretend to drown

Slip off the dock

Do a belly flop in shallow water

Scuba dive in three-feet of water

Drink the water

Dive in shallow water

Swing off a vine and forget to let go

Try to swing off of a rope but miss and hit a tree

At a Hockey Game

Talk during the national anthem

Jump on the ice during a game

Root for the team you're against

Yell bad words

Try to get food for free

Lick the ice

Eat other people's popcorn

Throw things on the ice

Ride a hockey stick around like a horse

Dance on your seat

Yell at the refs

Throw extra pucks on the ice during the game

Break the hockey sticks

Try to catch the puck but break your finger

Wear shorts and a t-shirt

In a Car

Spill juice on the seat

Stand in the seat with muddy shoes

Throw things at the driver

Un-buckle your seatbelt

Stick your head out the window

Jump out the door while moving

Sit on top of the car

Text while driving

Blast your music driving past a baseball game

Go through a red light

Speed past a police car

Complain to the police that it was an orange light

Loudly rev your engine in the middle of the night

Bump your head on the roof

Have road rage

In a Spaceship

Shut off the power

Break the windows

Go into the sun

Press random buttons

Take off without a spacesuit

Eat all the food on the first day

Put in the wrong coordinates for earth

Take off at the wrong time

Fall asleep when the ship isn't on autopilot

Run out of water

Eat messy food in zero gravity

Contact angry aliens

Lie to your crew

Set your ship on fire

Bring spiders on board and let them escape

On the School Bus

Take over the driver's seat

Jump out the window

Steal other people's backpacks

Eat food left on the seat

Draw on the windows with marker

Tear the seats

Crawl under the seats

Stand while the bus is moving

Tell the driver he/she is a bad driver

Do your homework on the bus

Lay down on the seat

Open up the emergency door

Throw marbles out the window

Crawl on top of the seats

Try to get trucks to honk their horn

At a Park

Get stuck on the monkey bars

Get a burn on the slide

Draw on the slides

Leave trash on the ground

Walk after spinning and fall down

Slide down the slide when it is wet

Throw wood chips

Throw sand

Spin on the spinner toys too fast

Block the end of the slide

Burn yourself on hot metal toys

Jump off the swings

Slide down the slide head first

Jump off the high rope jungle gym

Knock over little kids

While Watching a Scary Movie

Scream and scare those around you

Throw popcorn everywhere

Run away

Faint

Throw the remote at the TV

Cover your eyes

Keep talking about how scared you are

Laugh at all the serious parts

Fake smile all the way through it

Fall asleep

Clutch someone so tightly you hurt them

Crawl under the couch

Cry puddles onto the couch

Lie and say you're not scared

Cover someone else's eyes

While at a Comedy Show

Jump on stage with the comedian

Tell your own jokes while seated in the crowd

Fake laugh

Heckle the comedian

Eat a bowl of pasta in the audience

Throw food at the comedian

Stomp your feet after every joke

Run up and down the aisles during the show

Cry after a funny joke

Scream gibberish

Clap at inappropriate times

Talk on the phone

Laugh obnoxiously

Crawl on the seats like a lizard

Keep getting up to use the bathroom

While Vacuuming

Shred the plastic of the vacuum cord

Run over your toes

Vacuum up the cord

Try to vacuum on pavement

Pull the cord out of the outlet

Vacuum up small animals

Dump the bag/filter on purpose

Vacuum everything in your way

Vacuum up a bobbypin

Get your clothes stuck in the nozzle

Vacuum nails in a workshop

Clog every hole with dirt

Play with the nozzles

Keep turning it on and off on and off

Try to vacuum in the bathtub

During a Test

Start singing very loudly

Freak out

Tell someone an answer in code

Spill water on your test on purpose

Fill in every answer on multiple choice

Cheat

Pour chocolate syrup on your test

Jump up and down

Turn your test into a paper airplane

Get all the answers wrong on purpose

Put an A on your test before you even turn it in

Forget to study

Grade your test

Eat the test

Don't put your name on the test

While Swimming in an Ocean

Try to eat fish while they're swimming

Drink the water

Pet dangerous sea creatures

Swim too deep

Step on stingrays

Swim near sharp rocks

Take a breath underwater

Hug an electric eel

Run on slippery rocks

Get your hand stuck underwater

Use a cracked mask

Pretend you're a mermaid

Swim to a fishing boat and climb on board

Take a selfie with an angry shark

Wear heavy boots

Shoe Shopping

Buy shoes that are too small

Come in the store with stinky socks

Make a knot that you can't get out

Buy high heels that are impossible to walk in

Buy shoes without looking at the price

Buy every shoe in the store

"Accidentally" spit in the shoes

Break the heels

Try on new shoes then forget to pay

Spill coffee in the shoes you are trying on

Cut off the end of the shoes so they will fit

Walk out without shoelaces

Leave your dirty socks on the floor

Wad your socks into a ball and throw them

Forget your shoes that you bought

In an Ambulance

Jam out to your favorite song

Leave the back doors open and lose the stretcher

Play with all the buttons

Jump out the back while moving

Cause accidents

Sing opera when a patient is in the back

Text while driving

Pretend that you're a surgeon

Drive into another ambulance

Put on the sirens for no reason

Play darts with the shots of medicine

Bark out the window

Scream at people as you pass them

Pretend that you're driving an ice cream truck

Try to signal for trucks to honk their horn

Underwater

Forget your scuba gear

Stay under for as long as possible until you faint

Open your mouth

Try to drink a soda

Read a paperback book

Wear sunglasses instead of goggles

Dry yourself off

Hug a jellyfish

Hold someone underwater

Sing bad opera to dolphins

Play hide and seek with a shark

Eat a peanut butter & jelly sandwich

Paint

Poke holes in the bottom of boats

Have a staring contest with a shark

At a Movie

Talk on your phone

Create a soda river on the floor

Never stop talking

Stuff food in the seats

Pour liquid in the cup holder

Bring several babies into the theater

Throw all of your popcorn at the screen

Watch a movie on your phone

Ask for a cup of butter

Dance in the front of the screen

Smoke in the theater

Light the screen on fire

Bring a five year old to a rated R movie

Yell in the middle of a movie

Spoil the movie before the movie starts

While Babysitting

Leave the kids and go take a run

Forget to feed the kids

Lock the kids in their rooms

Play on your phone and ignore the kids

Lock the kids in the basement

Have a huge party

Feed the kids the cat's food

Teach the kids how to smoke

Let them watch violent movies

Feed the kids only junk food

Let them watch as many movies as they want

Feed them till they barf

Let them color on the walls

Play paintball in the living room

Give them all crazy haircuts

On a Holiday

Ask everybody if they got you gifts

Wrap up a pile of rocks

Open the gifts before you're supposed to

Wake up late and miss opening gifts

Try to catch Santa Claus

Open other people's gifts for them

Throw everyone's presents in the fireplace

Cry if you don't like a gift someone gave you

Wrap a random box with nothing in it

Unwrap and then re-wrap your presents

Buy someone a gift then keep it for yourself

Yell if you hear something and wake everyone up

Hide other kids' gifts

Trap the Easter Bunny

Give someone a bag of dirt wrapped in pretty paper

While Cooking Dinner

Set the food on fire

Forget to wash your hands

Leave something in the oven overnight

Set the grill on fire

Forget to take the wrappers off of food

Put anchovies in everything

Serve some food raw that shouldn't be

Allow preschoolers to run the kitchen

Cook only super smelly food

Let your pets lick the food before serving it

Refuse to do any cleanup

Add way too much salt

Overspice the food so it's ridiculously hot

Stir all the food with your hand

Break a glass over the food to be served

While eating dinner

Have a temper tantrum

Refuse to use your hands

Have an awkward silence

Start a food fight

Dump your water glass on someone's head

Text with people across the table

Bring loud toys to the table

Stuff as much food as you can into your mouth

Spit food into your glass of water

Chew your food very loudly

Tell disgusting stories that gross people out

Refuse to eat your food because it's not purple

When eating meat, give the meat a name and cry

Demand seconds, but don't eat anything else

Tell the cook the food is terrible

While Playing In The Mud

Stick mud in your ears

Eat the mud

Splash other people around you with mud

Wear brand new shoes

Put mud on a freshly mowed lawn

Put mud up your nose

Get mud under your fingernails

Use your phone in the mud

Dip strawberries in the mud like it's chocolate

Try to snorkel in the mud

Come in house and sit on a white couch

Roll on the carpet

Brush your teeth with mud

Hug your parents while covered in mud

Pretend to be a pig

Going Through Airport Security

Hide a Swiss-army knife in your mouth

Keep saying the word "terrorist" over and over

Bring a homemade clock that looks like a bomb

Look and act really nervous

Tell security that they are bad at their job

Wear a metal shirt

Yell at everyone in front of you to hurry up

Refuse to let them check your backpack

Look super suspicious

Wear a razor blade necklace

Bring a metal water gun

Climb on the metal detector

Wear shoes shaped like samurai swords

Roll metal marbles through the metal detector

Dance in the body scanner

At a Basketball Game

Do yoga at center court

Jump out of the stands and steal the basketball

Sit on the bench even though you're just a fan

Throw food at the referee

Play defense on the refs

Throw a paper airplane on the court

Light a firecracker when a player is shooting

Climb on the hoop

Rush onto the court every time the whistle blows

Use scissors to cut down the net at halftime

Throw another basketball on the court

Pour water on the floor to make everyone slip

Go in the locker room and steal the players' clothes

Sing Happy Birthday during the national anthem

Tie player's shoelaces together during a timeout

At the Super Bowl

Dance on the field

Dump water on the coaches for no reason

Eat food you are allergic to

Root for a team not playing

Parachute onto the field

Bring a giant banner, blocking people's view

Throw food at the players

Set the grass on fire

Bring your pet skunk

Sneak into the locker room at halftime

Steal the trophy

Deflate the football

Steal the Super Bowl rings

Drop food on the person's head in front of you

Run onto the field and tackle a player

At a Dance Party

Spill soda on other people

Try to crowd surf

Go crazy and accidentally jump out a window

Take over as DJ and play nursery rhymes

Take a nap on the dance floor

Dance with people who don't want to dance

Crash someone else's party

Pour slippery dish detergent on the floor

Punch a hole in the speakers

Dance so wildly that other people get hurt

Start singing your own song

Take food that is there and then leave

Jump on other people's backs

Stick your face in the punch bowl

Start a conga line

While Running a Marathon

Sprint the first five miles then faint

Wear a super warm monkey suit

Take breaks every 30 seconds

Take your water bottle and throw it at somebody

Skip the whole way

Wear flip flops

Run with your shoes untied

Baby step to the finish line

Try to run the slowest marathon

Trip on the person in front of you

Kick someone with your running shoes

Not budge from the starting line

Take water cups from fans and throw it at them

Drink nothing but chocolate milk

Run with your pet lion

While Skydiving

Forget your parachute

Eat a box of cookies

Fall asleep

Jump out of the plane too early

Drink a milkshake

Use a knife to cut the parachute when it opens

Jump into someone else's open parachute

Forget to wear warm clothes

Text while jumping

Jump into the engine

Land in shark infested waters

Drop your phone

Use a broken parachute

Try to use an umbrella as a parachute

Land in a prickly rose bush

While Planting

Eat the plant

Use a magnifying glass to catch the plant on fire

Drink all the water

Use toxic chemicals on the plant

Eat the fertilizer

Plant weeds

Pick the flowers from the plant

Eat live worms

Water the plants too much

Throw mulch all over the place

Drown the plant in water

Forget to put in the seeds

Dig up the plant by accident

Eat the mulch

Forget to water the plant

During a Birthday Party

Invite your own friends to someone's else's party

Eat all the cake before it's cut

Pie someone with the cake

Blow out the birthday kid's candles

Take just the goodie bag and leave

Forget to give a present

Take more than one goodie bag

Pretend you're the birthday boy/girl

Steal the presents

Sprinkle salt on the cake

Fight over sitting next to the birthday boy/girl

Dive on the piñata candy

Randomly show up when you're not invited

Tackle the piñata

Be mean to the birthday boy/girl

While Doing Magic

Lose the bunny

Set the stage on fire

Lose the person in the teleportation box

Teleport into a watermelon

Cut someone in half and leave the person that way

Forget how to do a trick

Get stuck underwater

Guess the wrong card someone picked

Fall off the stage

Whisper your secrets into the microphone

Teleport into a volcano

Accidentally push a trapdoor button on the floor

Forget you have a snake up your sleeve

Die while doing a magic trick

Accidentally reveal your secrets

CPSIA information can be obtained at www.ICGtesting.com
Printed in the USA
BVOW06s1226140716

455212BV00005B/16/P